Photomeditations

Photomeditations

by Carl J. Pfeifer

Thomas More Press
Chicago, Illinois

Special acknowledgments:

Many of these photographs and text meditations were distributed and published through NC News Service Syndicate © NC News, and are reprinted here by special permission. The title "Photomeditation" is registered at the U.S. Patent Office by NC News Service and is used by special permission.

ISBN 0-88347-079-9

To Janaan
whose poetic vision
and realistic faith
guide me to look
for Life in life
and Love in love.

Introduction

Photomeditations emerged from the convergence of three personal convictions. The first is my belief, rooted in the Judaeo-Christian tradition, that all of life is graced by the presence of the Creator. The second is that photography provides us with a unique means of uncovering the invisible presence of God in the visible world. And the third is that words are an irreplaceable means of interpreting life's mystery and the photographic image of life. Of all words, I find the Hebrew and Christian Scriptures an unsurpassed interpreter of life's richness, depth and beauty.

St. Paul long ago assured the Christian communities that the Creator's invisible power and divinity might be caught sight of in the visible world (Romans 1:20). In this he was but echoing the wisdom of the psalmists, prophets and sages of Israel, for whom the world was filled with visible evidence of the invisible God. Gerard Manley Hopkins, the English Jesuit poet, sums up this tradition of a graced universe. "The world," he writes, "is charged with the grandeur of God."

If that is true, then one of life's most enjoyable and challenging tasks is to learn to see the divine in the human, the marvelous in the monotonous. St. Ignatius Loyola draws on centuries of experience in describing this basically contemplative task as "learning to see God in all things." That is the understanding of prayer that inspires these photomeditations.

I have found photography a significant help in the prayerful search for God in the world of daily experience. For photography encourages one to look at life more sensitively. The particular genius of photography, in the words of one of the greatest of photographers, Alfred Stieglitz, is its ability "to make visible the invisible."

A photograph has the unique power to capture a fleeting experience, to stop a moment of life so that we can gaze at it at length and savor its richness and depth. Photos, by their impact and immediacy, can help us grow from a superficial looking at life to a deeper seeing into life. A photograph can lead one through sight to insight.

In so far as a photo brings us a glimpse of life, it has the potential of helping us see the Creator in whom "we live and move and have our being" (Acts 17:28). A photo may thus become a rich resource for meditation, contemplation, prayer. In helping us see life with an awakening eye, photos can help us learn to see the unseen God in the world that we see.

Confucius already perceived in ages past that "a picture is worth a thousand words." Yet a word may just as truly be worth a thousand pictures or photos. Together, word and picture seem to find their fullest potential, with each interpreting, confronting, nuancing the other. Few words offer the depth of insight and the beauty of expression found in the biblical words. For Jews and Christians the scriptural words convey God's own word.

Photomeditations are my attempt to look at life through a camera and with a typewriter and to share with others my limited vision of the Creator in his multi-faceted, fascinating world. The photos attempt to capture unstaged, unposed moments of life that have caught my eye and heart. The words are my reflection on that aspect of life frozen by each photo and uniquely interpreted by the Scriptures.

Is is my hope that these photomeditations may stimulate your search for the invisible God in the world you see and encourage you in the art of seeing God in all things.

Arlington, Virginia
January 6, 1977

Wondering

A young woman sits inside a darkened room . . . looking out the window . . . her head resting in her cupped hands . . . as she gazes steadily at the world outside . . . wondering.

Wondering perhaps at what is happening in her life . . . or at what the future holds . . . concerned, maybe, about the emerging shape of her experience . . . or just wondering at the marvels . . . and mysteries of life.

It is good to pause at times . . . to look quietly at our inner and outer worlds . . . to take time to wonder at the mystery of it all . . . of birth and death . . . of youth and old age . . . of joy and sorrow . . . courage and fear . . . success and failure.

We tend to rush about . . . skimming the surface of our lives . . . failing to notice . . . to savor . . . to enjoy . . . to appreciate . . . to let our hearts and spirits fill with wonder . . . at the mysterious depths . . . and heights . . . and breadth of our experience.

Mary . . . the Gospels tell us . . . pondered in her heart . . . what was happening in her life . . . Like Mary . . . like this young woman at the window . . . we need to stop . . . to become still . . . to wonder at how extraordinary . . . the ordinary really is . . . to notice the traces of God's loving presence . . . just beneath the surface of our scattered lives.

Love and Struggle

Five words on a wall . . . sum up a life . . . and say so much about life . . . yet people walk by without a glance.

"Cast away" . . . Who is he? . . . Or she? . . . One whose life is a lonely search . . . for self . . . for meaning . . . Someone touched by sadness . . . familiar with suffering . . . The signature might be of any one of millions of young . . . and not so young . . . searchers walking the byways of life . . . sensing themselves apart . . . cut off . . . cast away . . . from a secure but sterile society.

"Love and struggle . . . words of street wisdom . . . born of grappling with life's harsh realities . . . touching deep into the mystery of life . . . shared with anyone willing to take a moment . . . to glance up and read . . . and then to ponder . . . to wonder . . . to pray.

"Love and struggle" . . . not words of naive optimism . . . nor of pat piety . . . but of hopeful realism . . . proclaiming that love is the heart of living . . . that to love is not easy . . . but that it is worth the struggle.

Jesus said much the same thing . . . "Love!" . . . first yourself . . . then your neighbor as yourself . . . and God in all and above all (Matthew 22:37-38) . . . "Love, as I love," he said (John 15:12) . . . That's what life is all about . . . ultimately to live . . . is to love.

Jesus added . . . from experience . . . that love costs . . . An outcast himself . . . cast away . . . he felt the struggle . . . and the hurt . . . of loving radically . . . "Unless the grain of wheat die," He said, "it remains alone" (John 12:24) . . . sterile . . . unfruitful . . . unloving . . . To open one's heart to love . . . involves the daily struggle to die . . . to selfishness . . . which is another word for sin.

"Love and struggle" . . . words of realism . . . words of hope . . . words echoing Jesus' call . . . from the cross . . . a castaway . . . to live in love.

Love.
&
Struggle

CAST AWAY

Joy in Work

A man at work . . . selling fruit in an outdoor market . . . apparently enjoying a customer's remark . . . and the warm sun.

His face radiates a sense of joy and well-being . . . an openness and at-ease-ness reinforced by his casual, open shirt . . . His hands . . . holding hard-earned dollar bills . . . are those of a working man . . . The whole scene conveys a warm . . . down-to-earth . . . joyfulness.

Joy in one's work . . . seems increasingly rare . . . in our world of assembly lines and office desks . . . ruled by relentless pressures of schedules and deadlines . . . There is a quiet appeal in the image of a smiling man . . . at work with the fruits of the earth . . . in familiar contact with people . . . a feeling of wholeness and simplicity and humanness . . . often missing from today's industrialized, bureaucratized businesses.

His laughter is a reminder that work is not meant to be a frustrating burden . . . nor a mindless means of achieving affluence . . . Christians share with Jews a deep respect for work . . . as a means of human fulfillment and fruitfulness . . . a source of joy and wholeness . . . and bonding between people . . . Human work and creativity are seen as a share in God's creative activity.

What can we do to enable ourselves . . . and more people . . . to find joy and satisfaction in work?

Anniversary

Jake and Anita celebrate 50 years of marriage . . . They cut a wedding cake together . . . just as they did half a century ago.

The ritual is the same . . . The cake is similar . . . but they have changed . . . Five decades of living have taken their toll . . . They are no longer the two dreamers . . . who cut the cake together on their wedding day.

In spite of age . . . or rather because of it . . . there is something even more beautiful . . . about golden jubilarians . . . than about attractive young brides and grooms . . . So much joy and sorrow . . . success and failure . . . pleasure and pain . . . are etched in their faces.

A golden anniversary celebrates the fulfillment . . . of what bride and groom romantically promised . . . It celebrates a bond of love . . . that has weathered the "better or worse" . . . the "richer or poorer" . . . for 2600 weeks . . . 18,262 days . . . 50 years . . . The "I do" . . . has become, "I have" . . . and . . . "I still do!"

Few images in life reveal more movingly . . . the richness of human love . . . than that of two people whose love has endured and deepened through five decades . . . Few experiences suggest more convincingly . . . the presence in human love . . . of a greater Love . . . a Love marked by unshakable fidelity . . . as well as by tenderness and affection.

Inner Eye

The eye . . .
window to the world . . .
mirror of the heart . . .
medium of learning . . . revealing . . . loving.
The eye . . .
marvelous lens . . . capturing life's colored
    forms . . .
sensitive reflector . . . of inner feeling . . .
delicate link between lovers.
The eye . . .
symbol of insight and contemplation . . .
symbol of inner vision . . . of one's life's light.
"The eye" . . . Jesus tells us . . .
"is the lamp of the body.
If your eye is sound . . .
    your whole body will be filled with light.
But if your eye is diseased . . .
    your whole body will be darkness . . .
If then, the light inside you is darkness . . .
    what darkness that will be!" (Matthew
        6:22-24).
Lord . . . we pray . . .
    that we may see . . .
        in your Light.

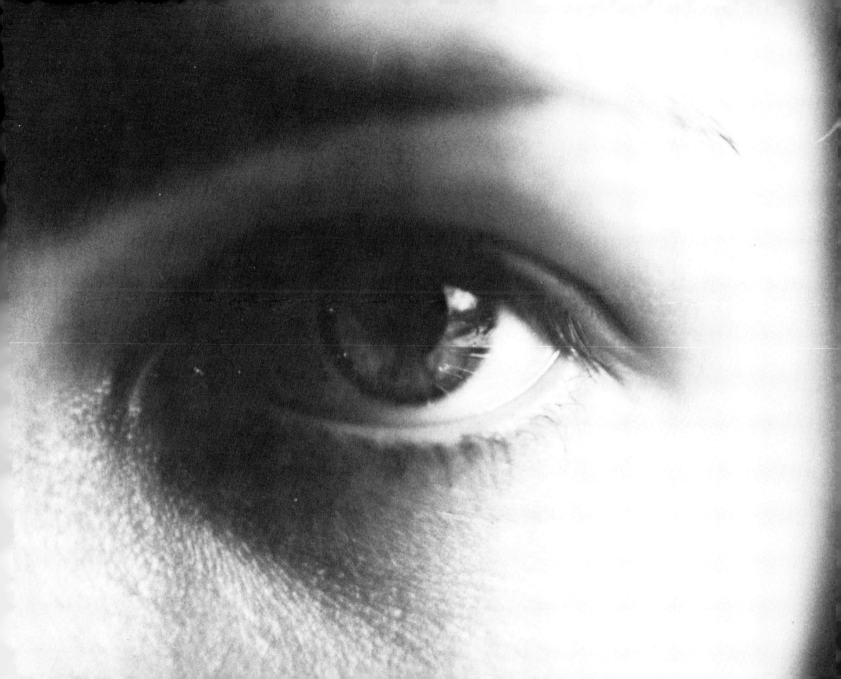

A Plea For Love

A rubbish can . . . scarred . . . dented . . . apparently kicked or pushed around . . . set apart from the building . . . not exactly attractive . . . The words painted so large and bold . . . seem to scream out . . . LOVE ME . . . The "ME" stands out brightest of all . . . in the sense of "even me" . . . The message really reads . . . "Please . . . love me . . . if you can!"

The painted rubbish can is symbolic of so many . . . who long to be loved . . . but feel unlovable . . . A gnawing sense of being unworthy of anyone's real care . . . gives rise to a yearning for love . . . while constantly frustrating or denying the approach of love.

The longing for love . . . mingled with a deep feeling of being unlovable . . . is one of the most common psychological agonies of our time . . . On a yet deeper level of experience . . . the painfully felt need to be loved . . . is at the heart of the mystery of life.

In a profound sense . . . all of us . . . even the most loved by family and friends . . . are in need of a mighty love . . . to make us whole . . . Selfishness . . . sinfulness . . . is rooted in the shadows of our being . . . At our more honest moments . . . we face the dents and scars . . . "original sin" . . . that even the greatest human love can not smooth or fill.

We sense our need . . . we experience a yearning . . . for Someone's love . . . to make us whole . . . and holy . . . to heal the scars and crookedness within us . . . to bring us inner peace, joy and beauty . . . to enable us to become the beautiful persons . . . we want to be . . . to make us truly lovable.

That sense of need . . . is what cracks open our hardened hearts . . . to allow God's love to enter in . . . Jesus praises the "poor in spirit" (Mt 5:3) . . . that is, "those who sense their need for God" . . . as "blessed" or "happy" . . .

Paradoxically . . . once the need of God's gracious, healing presence is sensed . . . then we can begin to recognize . . . that because of his love . . . we are lovable . . . in spite of our sinful scars and crookedness . . . Then the mystery of grace . . . can cause us to wonder with Saint Paul . . . at the marvel that Jesus . . . loved us and gave himself up for us . . . even though we are sinful (Gal 2:20).

Then, too, we can pray with Saint Augustine . . . "Lord, we are lovable . . . because you love us."

18

A Cemetery

A cold grey day . . . in a cemetery . . . The black earth hides the remains of the dead . . . remembered in cold, grey stone monuments . . . one of which is a cross . . . The black tree stretches out its leafless limbs . . . against a steel grey sky . . . The tree's tangled web of branchlets . . . heightens the sense of foreboding . . . and fear.

Death is a fearful reality . . . Black and grey are its instinctive colors . . . cold its spontaneous feeling . . . winter its natural season . . . Even the cross seems to share death's frigid starkness.

Yet the cross draws one's eye to it . . .

Something about it sparks an inner warmth . . . sheds an inkling of meaning . . . stirs a feeling of hope . . . For Christians the cross recalls death . . . in all its frightening reality . . . "Jesus died and was buried."

But the cross points beyond the grave . . . "On the third day he rose again from the dead."

The presence of the cross . . . cold and grey . . . in a wintry cemetery . . . reminds us that death is part of life . . . but that life is just as really a part of death . . . It wordlessly suggests what Vatican Council II proclaims . . . echoing twenty centuries of Christian experience . . . "Through Christ and in Christ . . . the riddles of sorrow and death . . . grow meaningful."

Life's Footsteps

Three footprints in the sand . . . made by strollers along the ocean shore . . . symbolize life's incessant journey.

We move on . . . one step after another . . . The footprints of the past . . . have long been washed away . . . No future prints are yet visible . . . We walk always in the present . . . never wholly free of past step's sands . . . not sure what the next step will bring . . . or even if there will be another step.

On so unpredictable a journey . . . what really counts . . . as we continue to walk on? . . . What is important? . . . What can we always take with us along the way . . . to help uncover the meaning . . . and share the beauty . . . of life's passing footsteps?

The Hebrew prophet, Micah . . . walked life's sands . . . centuries before Jesus . . . He gives us the fruit of his rich experience:

"This is what God asks of you . . . only this:

to act justly . . .
to love tenderly . . . and
to walk humbly with your God"

Micah 6:8).

Praise!

The sun peeks over rolling hills . . . its first rays glistening the placid lake . . . falling upon a young girl . . . who stands with arms raised in prayer . . . a silent prayer of praise.

Her silhouetted figure suggests a sense of wonder . . . wonder welling up through the body into a gesture of praise . . .

Praise of Light . . . whose awesome beauty . . . radiates through the sun's warm rays . . . dissolving darkness and the night's fears . . .

Praise of Life . . . whose vitality pulsates through the tingling excitement . . . of the first glimpse of dawn . . .

Praise of Love . . . whose warm presence is sensed . . . through the gentle touch of the sun's lengthening fingers . . . easing away the chill of night.

This young worshiper's morning gesture of praise . . . captures the praise of the Psalmist . . . who sings of the presence of the Creator . . . in sun and sky . . . wind, woods and waters . . . hills and valleys . . . and most of all in those who raise their hearts and hands in praise . . .

"Praise the Lord, O my soul;
    I will praise the Lord all my life;
    I will sing praise to my God while I live."
Psalm 146:2

A Sense of Wonder

Jerry lies on the garage floor . . . totally absorbed in an experiment . . . trying to burn a leaf with the sun's rays and a piece of glass . . . He is creatively exploring reality . . . testing how it works . . . caught up in its mystery.

His total absorption with his creative task . . . suggests something of a child's capacity to be captivated by reality . . . to wonder at its mysterious workings . . . to want to get involved with its creative processes.

Unfortunately as we grow up . . . and become busy about many things . . . we seem to lose that childlike openness and wonder . . . We tend to live on the surface of things . . . hurried . . . preoccupied . . . dulled to the marvels of the world in which we rush about

. . . no longer entranced by the mysterious power of sunrays and glass to spark a dead leaf.

Our hurried inability to stop . . . look . . . enjoy . . . wonder at the marvelous . . . mysterious world . . . betrays the best of our traditions as believers . . . Jesus, the prophets and psalmists before him . . . and millions of Christians after him . . . wondered at the beauty . . . the ugliness . . . the mysteries . . . of the universe . . . and found that their wonder . . . nurtured their faith . . . for they sensed everywhere traces of the divine presence . . . They found the Creator . . . in the marvels of creation.

Perhaps that is why Jesus once took a child . . . like Jerry . . . and said "of such is the kingdom of God . . . unless you become like a child . . . you cannot even enter God's kingdom" (Matthew 18:3).

Life's Paradox

A driftwood crucifix ... on a sandy shore ... stands out against the dark shadows ... firmly rooted in bright sunlight ... a sign of death ... become a symbol of life ... an instrument of darkness ... become a source of light.

Two wire butterflies ... symbolize new life ... creativity ... beauty ... born of death's drab cocoon ... The wire figure of the Crucified ... speaks of life's victory over death ... of light transforming darkness.

Every death contains seeds of life ... and no life is born but through dying ... Darkness is needed to see the light ... which illumines life's shadows ... without removing them.

A life without daily dying is deadly ... Light without shade blinds.

The mystery of the cross ... is the deepest mystery of life.

28

Pondering

She sits silent and alone . . . chilled by the winter wind brushing her dark hair . . . as she looks straight ahead . . . into the future . . . wondering . . . pondering.

Tangled shadows of barren branches . . . suggest life's criss-crossing, chaotic pattern . . . In the midst of the mysterious mass of interweaving dark shadows . . . she seems to possess a somber sense of inner peace.

Huddled against the chilling breezes of life . . . she . . . like all of us at times . . . seems to ponder in her heart . . . what it all means . . . what the future will bring . . . how to find one's way.

The brightness of her coat . . . reveals the presence of the sun . . . whose light reaches even into the tangled shadows . . . and whose warmth creates a sense of wholeness . . . and courage.

Like Mary . . . who pondered life's mysteries (Luke 2:52) . . . we all need silent times . . . quiet moments . . . to sense the warmth of God's presence . . . in the midst of life's cold winds . . . and to see the light . . . that is Jesus . . . reaching into life's tangled, shadowed paths . . . "There is a time to be silent" (Eccles. 3:7).

Between Life and Death

A busy city street . . . a man lies helpless on the ground . . . the victim of an accident . . . or a seizure . . . Two strangers kneel by him . . . as an ambulance approaches.

A moment . . . between life and death.

A moment . . . to view life . . . through the eyes of death.

A moment . . . that pierces the fog . . . of daily illusion . . . that removes life's masks . . . a moment that challenges . . . our assumptions and values.

At such a moment . . . that may be anytime . . . for any of us . . . what is really important? . . . What would I most fear losing? . . . What would I think of how I lived? . . . What would I wish I could change? . . . For what would I want to live? . . . Who would miss me? . . . Who would care if I lived or died?

At such a moment . . . Jesus' question of ultimate value . . . becomes unavoidable:

"What profit does a man show . . . who gains the whole world . . . and destroys himself in the process? . . . What can a man offer . . . in exchange for his life?" (Mark 8:36-37).

32

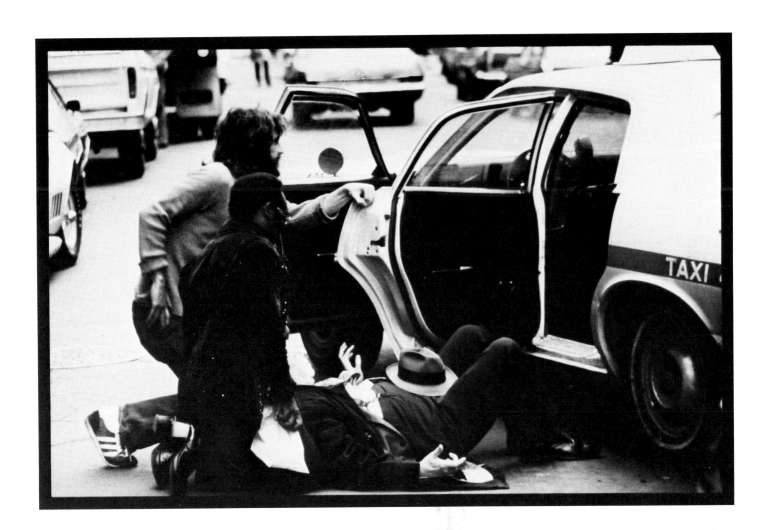

Jesus Laughed

Jesus laughed! . . . an interesting topic for a Sunday sermon. We might be led to wonder what Jesus laughed at? . . . or laughs at today.

Perhaps he laughs at us . . . as reflected in the glass . . . bustling about our cities in cars and buses . . . with only the parking meter reminding us of the shortness and sacredness of time . . . Or, like the young man sitting somberly on the steps . . . letting time slip steadily by.

What Jesus laughed or laughs at is less worth noting than the fact that he did laugh . . . to remind us that Jesus had a sense of humor . . . Didn't he once say that he came to share his joy with us? . . . Was it just an acci-dent that his first miraculous sign took place at a wedding party . . . where he replenished the wine supply? . . . Did not St. Paul assure us that Jesus was like us in everything . . . with the exception of sin . . . ? Of course he laughed!

But how many paintings or statues are there showing a laughing Savior? . . . Where in our devotions are there prayers to a laughing Christ? . . . We seem most easily to recall him as a "man of sorrows," . . . forgetting often how much joy his presence brought children and sinners, tax-collectors and party-goers, sick and dying.

Jesus laughed! . . . We can be sure of that . . . And he probably laughs at us . . . who rob religion of its playfulness . . . and remember him as a man of tears . . . rather than a person of smiles and laughter.

34

Death With Hope

Row after row of tombstones . . . fading off into a distant cold sea of stone . . . mute monuments to our mortality . . . recall the dead . . . and remind the living . . . that we too must someday die.

Amidst the shadowed marble memorials to the named and nameless dead . . . one stone shines in the sun . . . with a single word . . . HOPE . . . Someone whose name was Hope . . . lies remembered by a stone that proclaims . . . more than his or her name . . . HOPE.

How can there be hope . . . in a graveyard . . . surrounded by harsh evidence of the all-embracing reality of death?

For many, death is seen as the end . . . of pleasure . . . of family bonds . . . of power . . . of love . . . of life . . . of everything . . . After death . . . nothing.

For Christians . . . and millions of other believers . . . death is an end . . . but also a beginning . . . a time for weeping . . . but for rejoicing as well . . . a fearful moment . . . but one full of hope . . . Hope arises from faith in a God . . . who is a life-loving God of the living . . . a God whose love of life . . . and of people . . . led Him to embrace death . . . on a cross . . . that with Him . . . all might rise from death . . . to new life.

For those who know and love the living God . . . and His risen Son . . . who still bears on his body the marks of death . . . for such believers . . . death is really a fearful . . . yet hope-filled transformation of life.

As Jesus said . . . "Unless the grain of wheat dies . . . it remains alone . . . but if it dies . . . it generates new life" (John 12:24) . . . All dying hides in its mysterious shadows . . . the fruitful seeds of richer life . . . Death is the labor pains of a new birth . . . Death is the drab cocoon that brings forth the radiant butterfly . . . Even in the midst of death . . . there is . . . HOPE.

Stillness

A woman walks alone . . . along the ocean shore . . . on a cool, brisk day . . . The few gentle waves . . . and the smooth expanse of sand . . . suggest a calm peacefulness.

To walk alone at times . . . can be a healing experience . . . away from pressures of work . . . and pressing relationships of family and friends . . . alone with one's thoughts and feelings . . . alone with nature's freshness.

To be alone . . . need not be lonely . . . In fact, being alone at times nurtures deeper bonds . . . with one's innermost self . . . with others . . . with nature . . . and with one's God.

Quiet times alone . . . when we are peacefully in touch with ourselves and the world . . . can be special moments of sensing . . . that we are never alone . . . that we are loved . . . by Someone who is always with us . . . even when all alone along an empty beach.

Stillness is a sacrament . . . a sign amidst life's superficial scatteredness . . . of the presence of One . . . who bonds us with himself . . . with each other . . . and with the world.

Joy

His face radiates joy . . . surrounded by the smiles on his balloons . . . But his face . . . like the dark, smileless balloons . . . suggests that life is not all smiles . . . that there are mysterious pockets of shadow . . . of darkness . . . of pain . . . in his and everyone's life.

Still he smiles . . . symbolizing a joy that can fill the ups and downs of daily life . . . His smile and that of his balloons . . . suggest the joy one sometimes meets in people . . . who love much . . . enjoy much . . . and suffer much . . . a joy Jesus says He came to share . . . with anyone willing to trust him.

Joy . . . for Saint Paul . . . is a sign of the presence of Christ's Spirit . . . the Holy Spirit (Gal 5:22) . . . The joy of Christ is not a joyfulness that bubbles over the surface of life . . . not a plastic smile that covers an inability to enjoy life deeply . . . but a joy that finds its source deep within one's heart . . . where one senses the presence of Someone greater than any experience . . . yet part of every experience.

True joy arises . . . in times of happiness or sorrow . . . success or failure . . . from being aware of a mysterious but real presence . . . walking with one along life's myriad ways . . . Joy is rooted in the unshakable faith-conviction . . . that Christ Jesus loves us . . . that his Spirit is with us.

Christian joy is nourished on the awareness . . . that "neither death nor life . . . neither the present nor the future . . . neither height nor depth . . . nor any other creature . . . will be able to separate us from the love of God . . . that comes to us in Christ Jesus, our Lord" (Romans 8:38-39).

So . . . put a smile in your heart . . . and on your face . . . and "Rejoice in the Lord always! . . . The Lord is near" (Phil 4:4).

Love's Paradox

Love . . . scratched in the soft sand . . . as the ocean waters inch toward it . . . and the setting sun threatens to hide it in lengthening shadows . . . Footprints in the sand . . . made by the passing scribes of love.

It seems a paradox . . . Love is so fragile . . . so subject to the shifting sands of time . . . so affected by the ebb and flow of feeling . . . so touched by the lengthening shadows of life approaching death.

Yet love is of all things the most stable . . . the most unshifting and unsubmergible . . . True love endures light and dark . . . through the rhythmic tides of life . . . Love lasts longer even than the footprints of the lovers themselves . . . imprinted in the sand of a brief lifetime . . . Love is stronger than death.

Saint Paul praises love's enduring qualities in one of the most beautiful of all hymns to love . . . "There is no limit to love's power to endure . . . Love never fails . . . There are in the end three things that last . . . faith . . . hope . . . and love . . . and the greatest of these is love" (Corinthians 13).

Yet love takes root and grows . . . in the fragile, shifting soil of the human heart . . . subject to the ever changing climate of human experience . . . Love's endurability . . . in so fickle an environment . . . suggests the presence of God . . . who is Love . . . incarnate in human flesh.

Reverence for Life

A tiny bird . . . fell to the ground, nest and all . . . Stunned, the small creature trembled with terror.

A young boy . . . noticed the frightened fledgling . . . picked up bird and nest . . . and carried them gently in his hand . . . awed at the fragile life . . . pulsating in that small feathered being.

His hand . . . cupped to support the bird in its nest . . . suggests a reverence for life . . . that deserves pondering . . . He might have left the bird where it fell . . . or even killed it . . . but he carried it about . . . not knowing quite what to do for the bird . . . but reverencing it as a living creature.

In a violent age . . . this boy's gentle reverence . . . reflects an attitude . . . profoundly religious in its roots . . . that sees all of life as somehow sacred . . . awesome.

His reverence . . . recalls that of Jesus . . . who approached life with sensitive compassion . . . remembering Jesus' responsiveness to all who were in need . . . The Gospels describe him in poetic words . . . borrowed from the Hebrew prophet, Isaiah:

"The bruised reed he will not crush;
The smoldering wick he will not quench."
(Matthew 12:20; Isaiah 42:3

Beauty, Creation, Revelation

An attractive young woman and a sweet-scented magnolia blossom . . . a human being captivated by the beauty and scent of a flower . . . A face and a blossom . . . suggesting a profoundly mysterious relationship . . . between humanity and nature . . . a relationship pregnant with pleasure and pain . . . a relationship whose depths open out to the Creator.

A flower . . . a sacrament? . . . revealing the hidden beauty of God . . . making present His attractiveness . . . stirring a life expanding joy . . . in the heart of someone sensitive enough to notice . . . Men and women of faith . . . so the Bible tells us . . . noticed in the stars the awesome attractiveness of God . . . They sensed His calming presence in the still, quiet breeze . . . The sun and moon revealed His faithfulness . . . His absolutely dependable love . . . The mighty storm winds spoke of His powerful presence . . . Cool refreshing waters were a sign of His life-giving Spirit . . .

Believers caught sight of Him in the beauty of nature . . . a constant reminder of the transcendent, mighty, gentle Creator . . . intimately present . . . in the world he shaped . . . a lovably loving . . . enticingly attractive . . . mysteriously powerful Person.

God is so close . . . His presence is almost sensed . . . glimpsed . . . touched in the mysterious beauty and power of nature . . . Yet we tend to be blind . . . deaf . . . insensitive . . . to His presence . . . We fail to notice . . . taken up with ourselves . . . our works . . . We are busy . . . controlling . . . using . . . even destroying nature . . . We need God's help to open our eyes . . . to sensitize our heart . . . our mind . . . so we can stand in awe . . . or stop to enjoy . . . or pause in wonder . . . or thrill to a fresh experience.

If only we are open to Him . . . God's Spirit can gently renew our senses and spirit . . . to notice and respond to the Creator . . . trying to catch our attention . . . in the daily miracles, great and small . . . that fill the world.

A woman . . . a flower . . . humanity . . . nature . . . and God . . . Lord, that I may see!

Trust

Little Robert rests comfortably between his father's legs . . . seemingly at peace . . . calm and confident . . . as his father looks at him . . . with pride and love.

The sheer size of the father . . . in contrast with Robert's smallness . . . conveys a sense of power . . . but a power tempered by tenderness . . . a gentle strength that makes possible a calm confidence . . . within the child . . . who stands on his own feet . . . while enjoying the secure support of his father's massive legs.

Together, the two convey such a feeling of peaceful strength . . . and secure affection . . . that they present a visual ideal . . . of what it really means to be a father . . . and a son.

Robert's sense of at-home-ness . . . in the caring presence of his strong father . . . provides an example, too . . . of what St. Peter encourages us all to do . . . in regard to God, our Father . . .

"Cast all your cares on him . . . because he cares for you" (I Peter 5:7).

Undying Love

Mona and Bob . . . "forever" . . . Two lovers share with the world . . . a love they experience . . . as everlasting . . . Carved in wood . . . their profession of undying love . . . is an act of incredible faith . . . in the staying power of the bond . . . they now feel so strongly.

There is something about love . . . that grounds so unshakable a faith . . . that allows so optimistic a hope.

In the inspired biblical love-song . . . the Bride professes a love . . . like that of Mona for Bob . . . "Set me as a seal upon your heart . . . for love is stronger than death . . . Many waters cannot quench love . . . neither can floods drown it" (Song of Songs 8:6-7).

True love . . . shares in God's love for us . . . a love that never ceases . . . as He assures us . . . "I have loved you . . . with an everlasting love" (Jeremiah 31:3).

Human love . . . can be forever . . . because it is a sharing in . . . an expression of . . . the unquenchable love . . . of him whose eternal being . . . is . . . love.

"If we love one another . . . God dwells in us . . . and His love . . . is made perfect in us" (I John 4:12).

Evening of Life

The slanting lines of the window frames . . . seem to be closing in on this aging woman . . . just as life's opportunities . . . are steadily narrowing with each successive year . . . The black darkness inside the room . . . hints at the fearful aspects of gradual diminishment . . . as the light of life slowly dims.

Yet she seems alive with an inner strength . . . her body turned from the darkness . . . toward life . . . toward other people . . . her face fully in the light . . . her mouth and eyes still full of life . . . Her whole body seems set against the forces of death . . . that are closing in on her . . . She seems eager to keep a firm grasp on the life . . . that is evidently slipping away.

Growing old is a mysterious experience . . . rooted in the greater mystery of life and death . . . of good and evil . . . The men and women of the Bible saw old age as one of God's great blessings . . . They prayed to live a long life . . . enjoying the presence of their children and grandchildren . . . To be "full of years"

was a sign of God's special love.

But old age can seem more a curse than a blessing . . . in the modern Western world the elderly often experience poverty, loneliness, a sense of uselessness . . . which sap their ebbing energies more than do sickness or physical weakness . . . There can be a gnawing impatience with oneself . . . an enervating fear of the future . . . a hollow emptiness . . . a sense of being engulfed in darkness . . . as the light of life flickers.

The image of this little old woman . . . reflects the mystery of old age . . . without resolving it . . . The darkness is there . . . the walls continue to close in . . . but she takes a strong stand for life . . . for light . . . for love . . . She seems to find meaning . . . even in the face of weakness . . . sickness . . . old age . . . death.

She is a Christian . . . believing that diminishment and death . . . contain seeds of new life . . . that to share the sufferings of Christ . . . is to have a share in his resurrection . . . that ultimately life wins out over death . . . if one believes enough . . . to choose . . . life.

A Man Like Every Man . . . Or?

Hands on hips . . . a young man stands thinking . . . Christ seems to dominate his horizon . . . His T-shirt proclaims faith in Jesus Christ . . . as eternal life.

His stance suggests an inner pondering . . . a sense of wonder shared by all who seem to know Jesus Christ . . . a questioning felt already by Jesus' first disciples . . . who asked themselves . . . "What does this mean?" (Mark 1: 27) . . . "What sort of man is this?" (Mt 8:27).

The experience of Jesus Christ in one's life . . . and serious faith in Him . . . is always marked by wonder . . . questioning . . . awe . . . "What sort of man can this be?" (Lk 8:25)

Mighty in awesome power . . . "even the winds and sea obey Him" (Mt 8:27) . . . Jesus is at the same time sensitive and gentle . . . "the bruised reed He will not crush" (Mt 12:20).

He is a king who rules by serving . . . a priest at home with sinners . . . a prophet who remains awesomely apart . . . yet loves intimately . . . Jesus powerfully stills storms . . . yet is Himself engulfed in waves of inner anguish and fear . . . He heals others while being broken himself . . . loved and hated . . . persecuted and condemned . . . yet loving even to the end . . . He finds new life . . . in the ultimate agony of death.

Jesus Christ . . . a man like every man . . . while so much more than an ordinary man . . . asks each of us . . . "And you . . . who do you say that I am?" (Mt 16:15).

People Bridges

Hands . . . clasped . . . in affection . . . and trust . . . a bridge between two people.

"No man is an island," . . . wrote poet John Dunne . . . Yet everyone is an island . . . alive but isolated in a vast sea . . . peopled by millions of separate islands . . . buffeted by life's ups and downs . . . each ultimately alone.

We need bridges . . . between our separate existences . . . We need to reach out to others . . . even to discover and appreciate . . . our very uniqueness . . . and beauty . . . We need bridges with other persons . . . bridges of understanding . . . of acceptance . . . of trust . . . of love . . . to recognize the jewel . . . that is our island self.

Hands reaching out to another . . . clasping with sensitivity and strength . . . symbolize those people bridges . . . that enable us to discover our own worth . . . as we recognize the beauty of another . . . who genuinely cares . . . and we trust enough to share . . . a fleeting moment . . . or a lingering lifetime.

Hands clasped in mutual care . . . reveal the presence of Jesus Christ . . . our "pontifex" . . . our bridge-builder.

Friends

Two boys look into the camera . . . together
. . . One arm around the other's shoulder . . .
a quiet smile . . . a sense of pride and confidence . . . a warmth shared on a cold day
. . . They look at life . . . together . . . They are
friends.

Friends double the joy of life . . . and divide
its pain . . . by sharing both.

A friend is someone . . . who knows you as
you are . . . and still likes you . . . A friend is
someone . . . who affirms the best in you . . .
yet understands the worst in you . . . accept-
ing you as you are . . . while gently calling
forth in you . . . that part of you still strug-
gling to be born . . . the real you . . . the person you want to be . . . whom you hope to
become.

A friend looks at the mask of you . . . that
everyone else sees . . . yet looks behind it . . .
beneath it . . . because he loves and respects
you . . . He discovers you . . . because he loves
you.

These two young friends . . . call to mind
the words of wise men of old . . . Israel's
sages . . . "He who is a friend is always a
friend" (Proverbs 17:17) . . . "A faithful friend
is a sturdy shelter . . . he who finds one finds
a treasure . . . A faithful friend is beyond
price . . . no sum can balance his worth . . . A
faithful friend is a life-saving remedy . . . such
as he who fears God finds; . . . For he who
fears God behaves accordingly . . . and his
friend will be like himself" (Sirach 6:14-17).

National Shrine

The National Shrine of the Immaculate Conception in Washington, D.C. is a huge, impressive structure . . . inspiring a sense of awe . . . at its massiveness and grace.

But here the Shrine looks so small . . . almost threatened by the overpowering branch of the black tree . . . which seems menacingly to reach out its tangled tentacles . . . toward the Shrine.

The small but solid form of the Shrine . . . with its straight vertical lines . . . softened by the curves of the dome and chapels . . . glistening white in the bright sunlight . . . contrasts sharply with the ragged, tangled branches of the black tree . . . that seems to hover over it.

It suggests something of the mysterious presence of the Church in today's world . . . Is the Church to be a great, awesome, powerful reality . . . compelling admiration by its sheer size and influence? . . . Or is it to be a diminishing community . . . in an increasingly confused and menacing world? . . . A community that captures the imagination and affection of people . . . not by its numbers or money or power . . . but by the lives of its members . . . and the ideals they stand for . . . justice . . . honesty . . . reverence for life . . . concern for the poor and weak . . . mutual support and care . . . peace . . . joy . . . and love.

What is your image of the Church in today's world? . . . What image of the Church might Jesus feel more comfortable with?

Blindness is Not Seeing

Who is really blind? . . . The Gospels are peopled with blind men . . . begging to see . . . and with people who have good eyes . . . but cannot . . . or will not . . . see . . . Jesus suggests that we are all at least partially blind.

Blindness is not seeing . . . It is an affliction . . . less of the eyes . . . than of the heart . . . To be blind is to fail to notice the poor . . . to refuse to recognize the needy . . . to close one's eyes to injustice . . . and suffering.

To be blind is to walk through life . . . so preoccupied with self . . . as to miss life's mystery . . . its beauty and ugliness . . . its smiles and its tears . . . Blindness means seeing the splinter in another's eye . . . while overlooking the log in one's own.

Really blind people . . . do not recognize the extraordinary in the ordinary . . . They miss the marvelous within the monotonous . . . True blindness closes our eyes to the presence of One . . . who alone can open our eyes and hearts . . . to see deeply, sensitively, compassionately.

Blindess is selfishness . . . shading our eyes . . . locking our hearts.

Like the blind men of the Gospel . . . we all need to pray . . . "Lord, I want to see!" (Mark 10:51).

One Way

As I look quietly at this photo of a cemetery . . . my first reaction is to smile . . . at its obvious humor . . . The juxtaposition of the traffic sign and the tombstones catches my interest immediately . . . The obvious meaning of the sign . . . indicating a one-way drive . . . takes on another meaning . . . when viewed in the same glance with the tombstones . . . The resulting hint of humor in a photo of tombstones . . . suggests my mixed feelings about death.

Death is a one-way path . . . One who dies passes into the unknown . . . from which there is no return . . . The shadows surrounding the tombstones . . . find a resonance . . . in my deepest fears of dying . . . I do not want to die . . . Death remains veiled in mystery . . . engulfed in shadowy unknowns . . . Death is a one-way street . . . which most of us are profoundly hesitant to enter.

Yet I can smile in the face of death . . . The photo's touch of humor . . . stirs in me a feeling . . . that is even more profound . . . than my fear of death . . . I sense that death's one-way path . . . is not a dead-end . . . Death cannot be the end . . . I respond to the inner conviction . . . that death's mystery opens up . . . into a new life . . . a new kind of freedom . . . I have seen people die with a smile on their lips . . . I have watched grieving relatives . . . smile through their tears . . . I stood before Martin Luther King's tombstone . . . that proclaims my faith . . . "Free at last . . . thank God, I'm free at last."

With Christians of all ages . . . I believe that the human hope . . . of life beyond the grave . . . finds its deepest roots in the experience of Jesus Christ . . . He died . . . was buried . . . and yet was seen alive by his friends . . . after he had been buried . . . As I look at the photo . . . with its smiling invitation to face death's shadows . . . I recall the words of Jesus . . . "I am the resurrection and the life . . . whoever believes in me . . . though he should die . . . will come to life" (John 11:25) . . . I remember Paul's challenge to death . . . "Death is swallowed up in victory" . . . "O death, where is your victory? . . . O death, where is your sting?" (I Cor 15: 54-55).

A Potter's Skill

Skilled hands mold and shape . . . a glob of whirling clay . . . into an attractive, useful pot . . . a marvel of creative interaction between an artist . . . and a mound of formless clay.

The clay responds to the sensitive fingers . . . taking the shape they gently but firmly desire . . . It is pliable . . . at the disposition of the artists dream and skill . . . as her fingers bring out the clay's potential for beauty.

A potter at work shaping clay . . . is a beautiful symbol of our lives . . . sensitively shaped by a God . . . who sees in our ordinariness . . . a vision of beauty and usefulness . . . such as we scarcely suspect lies within us.

With a potter's wheel in mind . . . the great Hebrew prophet, Isaiah, prayed to God:

"Yet, O Lord, you are our father;
we are the clay and you are the potter;
we are all the work of your hands"
(Isaiah 64:7).

Whether we ever become what God dreams we might be . . . depends on how we respond to the gentle but firm pressures of his life-shaping Spirit . . . We can become brittle and break . . . like glass . . . Or remain supple . . . like clay . . . responding to the Spirit's sensitive, skillful shaping of our lives.

Prayer

Two young men . . . kneeling in a public park . . . praying . . . heads bowed . . . arms around each other's shoulders . . . a Bible at their knees . . . a cross on one's chest . . . a feeling of being burdened . . . needing help . . . The pole on the ground seems to suggest a heavy weight . . . bearing down on them . . . as they grapple with life.

They are a moving symbol . . . of trust . . . or faith . . . amidst a heavy, troubled world . . . To bow one's head . . . to kneel . . . before God . . . is a sign of strength . . . a step toward wholeness . . . Someone once wrote . . . that a person is never more fully human than when on one's knees before God . . . To reach out . . . to another human being . . . is a gesture of growth . . . The Bible notes that . . . a brother helped by a brother . . . is like a strong city (Proverbs 18:19).

Openness to God . . . and to one's brother or sister . . . seem to go together . . . Both pierce the wall of selfishness . . . self-centeredness . . . self-sufficiency . . . that the Bible names "sin".

Jesus reminds us that those people are truly happy . . . blest . . . who recognize their need for God . . . who are "poor in spirit" (Mt 5:3) . . . A hit-tune echoes Jesus' conviction . . . that people who need people are the luckiest people in the world.

To kneel before God . . . with an arm around one's brother . . . admitting . . . sharing . . . one's need of God . . . and of other people . . . capsulizes what Jesus' life and words are all about . . . "Love God," He said . . . "with all your heart . . . and love your neighbor as yourself" . . . That is His formula for happiness . . . and salvation . . . He invites us . . . to open our hearts to God, our Father . . . with unshakable trust . . . called faith . . . and to our brothers and sisters . . . in trust and care . . . taking upon our own shoulders . . . their burdens.

Saint Paul sums it all up . . . What really counts, he says . . . is "only faith . . . which expresses itself in love" (Galatians 5:6).

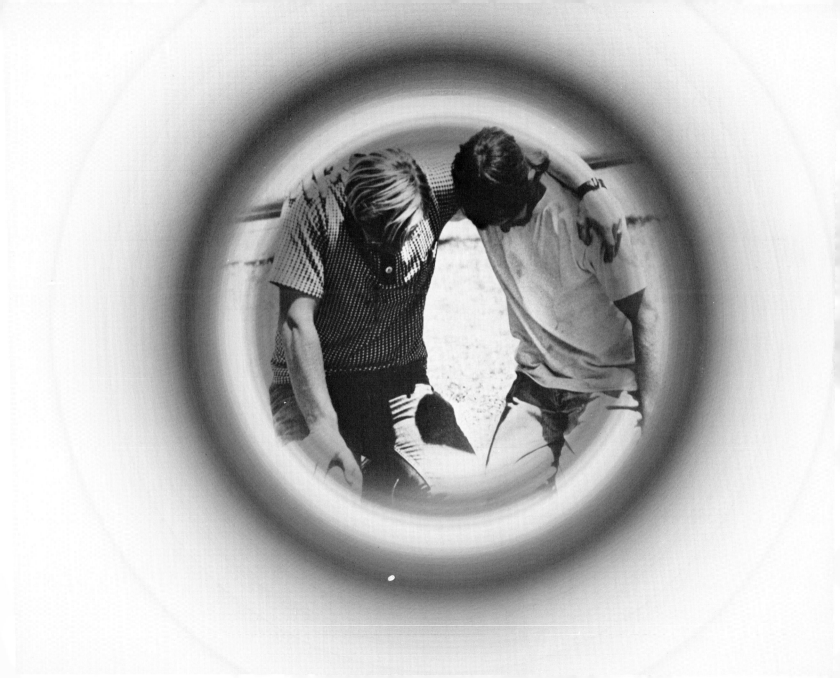

In Weakness, Strength

A man sits alone on a porch . . . apparently trying to clean or sand something . . . His bent position . . . his long arms and legs . . . seem caught in the strong downward movement of the metal railings . . . which create a feeling of "being down" . . . Black and grey edge out the white.

A closer look reveals two crutches leaning against the porch rail . . . and a metal brace on the man's right foot . . . He is crippled . . . The dreary, downward-pull of the scene . . . suggests an inner sense of being down.

Physical disability . . . sickness of body . . . tends to sap the spirit . . . muddle the mind . . . and depress the feelings . . . To be down bodily . . . pulls one's spirits down . . . Weakness of limb . . . gnaws inward . . . weakening the person . . . leading even to despair.

One of the most creative and challenging . . . paradoxical and puzzling . . . of Christian convictions . . . is that in weakness there can be found strength . . . Jesus told Paul . . . and he tells each of us . . . "My grace is enough for you . . . for in weakness power reaches perfection" (2 Corinthians 12:9).

Paul struggled with bodily and spiritual weakness . . . discovering in pain the truth of Jesus' words . . . Paul wrote what for him . . . and millions of Christians after him . . . were words of hope-creating conviction . . . "I willingly boast of my weaknesses . . . that the power of Christ may rest upon me . . . I am content with weakness . . . and difficulties . . . for the sake of Christ . . . for when I am powerless . . . it is then that I am strong" (2 Corinthians 12:9-10).

Unemployment

One woman's face . . . tells more about unemployment . . . than the latest statistics . . . Numbers, percentages remain abstract . . . impressive yet unmoving . . . true but cold . . . What is the difference between 8.3 per cent unemployed . . . and 8.5 percent?

Her face suggests the difference . . . in human hurt and humiliation . . . The sadness of her eyes reveals the hopelessness . . . of one person, one family, . . . whose pain is buried in statistical reports.

Surrounded by people . . . she seems alone . . . bewildered . . . Her sign . . . handwritten . . . seems to come straight from the heart . . . a cry . . . a plea . . . an urgent imperative rather than a polite request . . . "No more layoffs."

Few experiences hurt Americans more . . . according to recent research . . . than to be unemployed . . . A secure job is important . . . not just for food and rent . . . but for physical and emotional well-being . . . for a sense of dignity and self-respect.

In our days of widespread unemployment . . . this worried woman's face . . . and her scrawled plea . . . echo the call of Christ . . . to respond to those in need . . . What can we do to reduce unemployment? . . . What can we do to help those who are out of work?

Locked in Hell

A door . . . closed . . . two locks . . . a roughly painted inscription . . . "Hell."

Why? . . . What must life be like on the other side of the door? . . . What kind of frustration and hurt cry out from behind the door? . . . We can only guess . . . but "hell" can be anywhere.

The closed door . . . double-locked . . . symbolizes the loneliness . . . the self-contained anguish . . . the fearful closed-in-ness . . . that is "hell" . . . on earth . . . and afterwards.

"Hell" . . . can be wherever hatred strangles love . . . and locks the doors of one's heart . . . or real care even for oneself . . . "Hell" is wherever one's heart grows numb to one's need of God . . . and of other people . . . It is to be locked in upon oneself . . . not caring . . . not needing . . . not sharing . . . secluded in sterile selfishness.

Jesus stands at the closed doors of our hearts and knocks . . . inviting openness . . . "Here I stand . . . knocking at the door," he says . . . "If anyone hears me calling . . . and opens the door . . . I will enter his house . . . and have supper with him . . . and he with me" (Rev 3:20).

He knocks . . . not just once . . . but with the determined persistence . . . of one who loves . . . of one who can see behind the closed door . . . a lonely . . . frightened . . . frustrated . . . angry heart . . . His love invites . . . enables . . . one to open the door . . . at least a crack . . . to let love come in . . . but only if one chooses to do so.

"Hell" . . . forever . . . is coldly to refuse to open one's heart to him . . . or anyone . . . It is to prefer to lock oneself . . . into eternal loneliness.

Tears

Neil is crying . . . after a brief squabble with his brother, Thomas . . . who stands aside wondering . . . as caring adults move close to comfort and heal . . . An everyday happening in every family!

Yet Neil's tears symbolize the tears of everyone . . . and everything . . . A Roman poet centuries ago wrote about one of life's deepest mysteries . . . "Everything weeps," he noted . . . "Tears well up out of reality."

Why? . . . Why must children cry? . . . Why are tears so much a part of life? . . . Why is there pain . . . crying . . . hurting? . . . Tear drops symbolize the all-penetrating mystery of evil . . . so concealed in our hearts . . . so visible on the evening news . . . Why?

Evil's mystery . . . allows no neat answer . . . Tears do not admit of theological definition . . . nor scientific precision . . . A child's tears challenge the deceptive security of reason . . . as they open up life's shadowy depths.

Life's tears reveal our need . . . for others to respond with compassion and care . . . most of all for Someone stronger than evil . . . Who is present even in pain . . . Himself no stranger to suffering . . . Tears invite faith in a mighty God . . . who once wept . . . at a friend's grave . . . and in lonely anguish in a garden . . . as his friends slept.

Jesus tells us . . . from experience . . . that all dying contains seeds of new life . . . that suffering can lead to fulfillment and fruitfulness . . . that one can smile through tears . . . With Jesus . . . even the cross . . . can become a tree of life . . . while we look forward to that day . . . when "He shall wipe every tear from their eyes . . . and there shall be no more death or mourning . . . crying out or pain" (Rev 21:4).

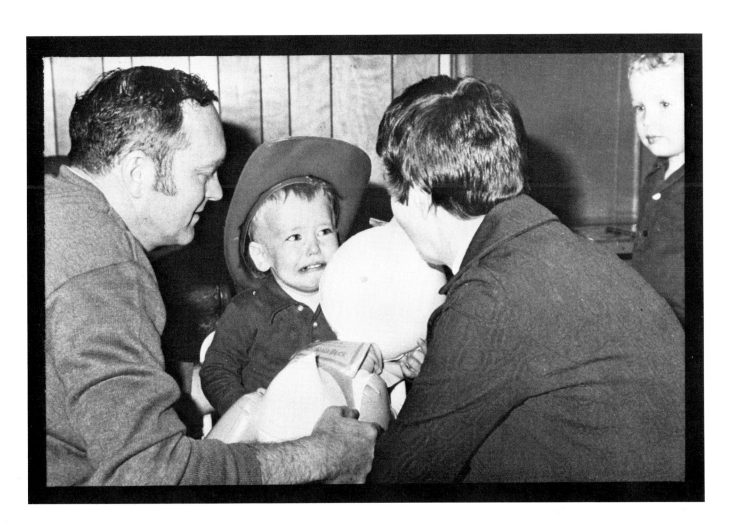

Forgiveness

Thomas kisses Neil . . . who a moment before was screaming . . . because Thomas had grabbed from him the rubber duck they now both clutch . . . They make up with a kiss . . . healing the fleeting hurt . . . saying without words . . . "I'm sorry!"

Thomas and Neil are brothers . . . They symbolize us all . . . brothers and sisters of the same Father . . . whose love gives us our very being.

Their kiss recalls the beautiful ideal of the Psalm . . . "How good . . . how delightful it is . . . for all to live together . . . like brothers" (Psalm 133:10).

Yet curiously we go on hurting each other . . . thoughtlessly . . . carelessly . . . even deliberately . . . The ideal is often so far from the reality.

Because we are the way we are . . . one of the very real signs of love . . . is to forgive . . . Jesus asks us to forgive over and over again . . . 70 times seven times . . . just as our Father keeps forgiving us.

Thomas and Neil making up with a kiss . . . remind us that . . . love means being able . . . and willing . . . to say, "I'm sorry!"

Open . . . But Rooted

The Gateway Arch in St. Louis . . . celebrates early America's openness to the frontier . . . It symbolizes openness to frontiers of every kind . . . A marvel of technological and artistic achievement, it suggests . . . the excitement . . . the challenge . . . the beauty . . . of opportunities that lie open to people in today's world.

The cross-peaked steeple of the Old Cathedral . . . the oldest Roman Catholic cathedral west of the Mississippi . . . celebrates the rootedness . . . the tradition . . . of American Catholicism . . . of world Christianity . . . The steeple points upward . . . but is solidly grounded . . . its cross . . . a symbol of Christian faith . . . rooted in twenty centuries' experience of Christ.

Together . . . Arch and Cross . . . symbolize the central tension of our time . . . of our Church . . . of millions of believers . . . How to be open to the future . . . to the world with its exciting opportunities . . . while remaining faithful . . . grounded . . . in our rich Christian tradition? . . . or . . . How to be faithful to Christ and his Church . . . while responding to genuine values in contemporary culture?

To deny or ignore modern developments . . . in science, art, medicine, psychology, technology . . . is to be unfaithful to the best of Catholic tradition . . . "Catholic" originally meant . . . "open to, embracing the whole world" . . . To forget or reject one's traditional Christian roots . . . is to deprive ourselves . . . and a torn, confused, uprooted world . . . of one of our richest sources of identity and meaning.

The challenge is . . . to be open and rooted . . . contemporary and traditional . . . to "read the signs of the times" . . . as Vatican Council II urges us . . . while interpreting them "in the light of the Gospel," . . . in the light of Christian tradition . . . and to reinterpret traditional meanings . . . in the light of new discoveries and insights.

Today's call . . . and that of every age . . . is to keep Arch and Cross . . . in a dynamic relationship . . . in creative tension.

Together . . . Apart

Four girls . . . a toy panda . . . at a carnival . . . together yet separate . . . Back to back each gazes off in a different direction . . . preoccupied . . . enclosed in her private world . . . There is a touch of sadness where one expects fun and laughter . . . A feeling of loneliness belies their physical closeness.

The photo conveys a common and painful experience . . . We long for community . . . togetherness . . . intimacy . . . but we often feel a gnawing, hollow loneliness . . . a separation from others . . . We are crowded by people . . . at work . . . at play . . . at home . . . yet something seems to distance us from each other . . . We remain enclosed in our separate worlds . . . gazing outward . . . but looking in . . . lonely . . . tinged with sadness.

Some mysterious force seems to wall us off . . . to narrow our world . . . to constrict our hearts . . . St. Paul named it SIN with a capital "S" . . . a power with a strong, subtle grip on our hearts . . . stifling love . . . sapping joyfulness . . . enclosing us in separate worlds . . . jamming real communication . . . fracturing relationships.

Jesus knew that experience . . . Surrounded by crowds, he was often profoundly alone . . . his life edged with sadness . . . He felt the distances . . . the separation . . . the tears of human experience . . . but struggled against that mysteriously centrifugal force . . . of self-centeredness . . . selfishness . . . that grips us all.

He opened his heart to everyone . . . He reached across the chasms between people . . . "A man of sorrows," He spread joy . . . He healed . . . bridged . . . united . . . Jesus' love broke through the alienation of Babel . . . through the lonely sadness of Calvary . . . to draw people close to himself . . . to each other . . . with joy . . . "I came to share my joy with you," He says . . . "that you may be at one as the Father and I are one" (John 15:11; 17:21-22).

Spirit of Jesus . . . help us . . . to crack the walls of our isolated hearts . . . to melt our cold defenses . . . to smile in our hearts and on our lips . . . to expand the small expense of our private little worlds . . . Where there is sadness, let us sow joy . . . Where there is separation, let us bring love.

Chains

A chain . . .
symbol of all that binds . . . and holds us captive.

There are chains of steel . . . solidly linked . . . seemingly unbreakable . . . chains that can shackle our arms and legs . . . holding us in physical bondage.

Still other chains . . . stronger and harsher . . . grip our minds and spirits . . . locking them in fear . . . ignorance . . . and selfishness . . . invisible chains shackling us from within . . . sometimes with our consent . . . most often against our will.

More vicious chains ring us round . . . in a tightening circle of poverty . . . prejudice . . . disease . . . exploitation . . . social bands that cripple the spirit . . . restrict creativity . . . and hinder growth.

Daily experience reveals our bondage . . . the evening news reports it . . . We are all enslaved . . . by chains we are helpless to break.

Into our bondage Jesus comes . . . as liberator . . . savior . . . He can set us free . . . He assures us:

"The Spirit of the Lord is upon me . . .
He has sent me to proclaim liberty to captives . . .
and release to prisoners"

(Luke 4:18).

Walking Alone

A young woman walks alone . . . on a chilly Sunday afternoon . . . The barren trees . . . the dark shadows . . . convey a sense of heaviness . . . The lines of the unpeopled walk . . . seem to narrow . . . as the shadowy trees appear gradually to close in.

Instead of walking into an expansive openness . . . she walks into what looks like a narrowing cave . . . The constricting lines and shadows . . . reflect the inner fear and oppressiveness . . . that is part of loneliness . . . as one walks into the future alone.

Loneliness tends to constrict the heart . . . to shade the spirit's vital spark . . . to limit dreams . . . and narrow expectations . . . Loneliness is a cancer of the spirit . . . ennervating . . . extinguishing.

Yet even when most alone . . . some strength . . . some hope . . . may come from knowing . . . that Someone walks with us . . . along life's shadowed paths . . . Someone who walked life's loneliest way . . . alone . . . who felt the fear . . . and tasted the sadness . . . whose way narrowed to a cross.

"I am with you always" . . . He assures us (Matthew 28:20).

An Invitation To Mystery

A long corrugated pipe . . . an invitation to mystery . . . a call to enter and explore . . . The boy begins to crawl in . . . curious . . . perhaps feeling some apprehension . . . not knowing just what might be inside . . . not sure where or how he may come out . . . but entering into a new experience.

It seems so much like life . . . Something draws us ever into the unknown . . . even as we enjoy the security of the known . . . Life is like that long pipe . . . its limits pressing in on all sides . . . its unknown length inviting us to enter more fully . . . into its uncertain promise.

Like the boy . . . we are usually apprehen-sive . . . What lies ahead? . . . How will it come out? . . . Many of us look into the shadowy future . . . and pull back . . . satisfied with what we have . . . with what we are.

But the invitation is always there . . . sometimes cloaked as curiosity . . . sometimes masked as escape . . . sometimes filled with desire . . . an invitation to live life more fully . . . a call to enter the darkness . . . unsure of the way or the distance or the direction . . . but confident of the light at the other end.

God calls to each of us . . . "I set before you life and death . . . choose life!" (Deuteronomy 30:19) . . . Don't hesitate to set forth with courage . . . or at least crawl in with anxiety . . . but don't hold back . . . "You have no need to fear . . . since I am with you . . . says the Lord" (Genesis 26:24).

Senior Citizens

Elderly men and women . . . sitting in a park . . . enjoying the sun's warmth on a mild, late-winter afternoon . . . They seem lost in their own thoughts . . . worried, lonely, weary . . . hoping the bright sunlight will banish for a time . . . the lengthening shadows of their waning lives.

Each seems preoccupied . . . with something fleeting that catches the eye . . . or with something deep inside that won't so easily go away . . . One finds escape in sleep . . . None seem aware of those beside them . . . sharing the same park bench . . . sharing the same sapping experience of growing old.

Old age and loneliness . . . seem common companions . . . in our country . . . where we speak euphemistically of "senior citizens" . . . but show the elderly so little real respect . . . so little honest concern.

If Jesus were speaking to us today . . . he might add to his great parable of judgment (Matthew 25:31-46) . . . "I was old, and feeling useless . . . and you ignored me" . . . Surprised we would ask . . . "Lord, when did we do anything like that? . . . When did we ignore you?" . . . His response could be . . . "Look around you . . . in your parks . . . in your apartment complexes . . . and nursing homes . . . perhaps in your own home . . . What you do to these elderly people . . . you do to me!"

Fragile but Enduring

Broken glass . . . a shattered window . . . jagged pieces fallen on rough, weather-worn boards . . . on the porch of an abandoned house.

The broken glass calls up images of shattered dreams . . . of ideals splintered against the harsh realities of life . . . of the brittle fragility of being human.

The rough boards . . . nailed in place, orderly and solid . . . worn but firm . . . provide rest for the fragile glass . . . Having endured the rigors of nature for long years . . . the seasoned boards suggest something of human durability . . . in the face of life's brokenness.

Life is like that . . . People are like that . . . fragile but firm . . . breakable yet able to endure . . . There is a mystery about life . . . about people . . . a mystery of strength in weakness . . . of something solid under the brittleness . . . of power to endure the fragmenting flow of time.

What is the source of that security . . . even when a life seems shattered? . . . What grounds people in hope . . . when everything seems to be breaking apart?

Whether we can name him or not . . . the enduring ground of our being . . . is our God . . . and His Son, Jesus Christ . . . in whom all things hold together . . . in whom we are ultimately rooted . . . in whose image we fragile humans are made.

Praying

A young man . . . kneeling upright . . . in a park . . . with other young people . . . praying . . . Not a common sight in city parks . . . but a moving one . . . Shirtless . . . with long hair . . . and torn shirts . . . he seems so calm . . . at peace . . . kneeling attentively in the hot sun . . . His long arms hang quietly . . . His head seems slightly raised . . . as if aware of a presence . . . greater than himself . . . There is a sense of wholeness . . . being together . . . a kind of openness . . . or readiness . . . to listen . . . and then to respond.

There is something beautiful about a young man praying . . . so unashamedly . . . on his knees in public . . . He becomes a kind of challenge . . . or attraction . . . inviting one to pray.

What is prayer? . . . Why pray? . . . This young man's whole body suggests what prayer is . . . a receptiveness . . . an openness . . . to Someone . . . greater . . . more gracious . . . than oneself . . . than the whole world . . .

Prayer is placing oneself . . . in the presence of . . . in tune with . . . God . . . "in whom we live . . . and move . . . and have our being" (Acts 17:28) . . . So St. Paul describes the all embracing reality of the divine . . . whose love . . . is the source of our life.

The young pray-er . . . recalls Moses . . . who removed his shoes and bowed to the ground . . . in God's presence . . . or Jesus . . . who prayed in solitude in the quiet hills . . . and surrounded by crowds in city streets . . . or a young girl, Mary . . . who stilled her whole being before her God . . . listened attentively to his invitation . . . and responded fully . . . "Behold the Lord's handmaid . . . do with me as you wish" (Luke 1:38).

94

Infinity

A gleaming monument to progress . . . The mathematical symbol of "infinity" . . . gracefully sculpted in silvery steel . . . set against the expansive sky . . . celebrates the seemingly unlimited potential of human creativity.

The streaking jet soars up into the open sky . . . piercing clouds . . . defying the earth's downward pull . . . symbolizing the adventurous spirit of humankind . . . ever straining to transcend the limits of finiteness.

Both jet and symbol gracefully speak of the inner restlessness of the human spirit . . . to break through all barriers . . . to grasp for the infinite . . . Both are signs of the presence of God's creative spirit . . . within the human heart . . . "When you send forth your Spirit" . . . sings the Psalmist . . . "you renew the face of the earth" (Psalm 104:30).

The dramatic modern breakthroughs of human creativity . . . deserve to be celebrated . . . They are a striking response to God's challenge . . . to create with him . . . a better world for people . . . They witness to the presence of the Infinite within our finite world.

We can safely look up with pride at what we have done . . . if we look ahead responsibly at what remains to be done . . . to break through barriers of ignorance, poverty and division . . . and look deep within to discover the source of our drive for the infinite . . . as Saint Augustine did . . . who prayed . . . "You have made us for yourself, O Lord, . . . and our hearts are restless until they rest in you."

A Mother's Love

A mother smiles at her toddler son . . . Her face radiates a love that is warm and positive . . . Her total affection for him is so obvious . . . so joyful . . . so attractive . . . Such love has the power to call up in a child . . . a sense of well-being . . . a contented assurance of being loved . . . of being lovable.

This mother's radiant smile . . . suggests the creative, calming power of love . . . It seems a perfect image of God's gracious regard for us . . . We are used to calling God "Father" . . . but a mother's love may better image God's love for us.

God is our "Mother", too . . . with all the tenderness . . . patience . . . expectancy of a mother for her loved child.

God says to each of us . . . through the words of the prophet Isaiah:

"Can a mother forget her infant? . . . be without tenderness for the child of her womb? . . . Even if she forgets . . . I will never forget you!"

(Isaiah 49:15).

Laws

A law . . . posted on a sign . . . may appear to restrict freedom . . . "Positively No Skating."

A second sign suggests the value . . . the law is meant to protect . . . life itself . . . "So Far This Year 10 People Have Drowned in This Area."

Both signs stir reflection . . . on the meaning of laws . . . Is an action good . . . because it is commanded? . . . bad because it is forbidden? . . . Or is an action to be commanded or forbidden . . . because it is already good or bad? . . . What gives a law authority? . . . the law itself and the lawgiver? . . . or the existing right or value . . . the law calls attention to and protects?

One's answer can have serious consequences for daily living . . . The first answer seems easier to live out . . . Learn the law and obey it . . . The second answer seems filled with painful decisions . . . Sometimes a law may endanger rather than protect a basic right or value . . . Perhaps obedience to the spirit of the law . . . leads to breaking the letter of the law.

Both attitudes toward law have risks . . . legalism in the first . . . diminished respect for authority in the second.

What is my attitude to laws?

How do I deal with law . . . in my own life?

The Past

An abandoned house . . . shattered windows
. . . black emptiness inside . . . weeds outside
. . . a silent reminder of the past.

How much living that old house sheltered!
. . . How many parties . . . How much laughter
. . . how many tears . . . It knew years of love
. . . and years of frustrations and challenges
. . . How much joy and peace? . . . Who can
tell?

The people who lived there have long
moved . . . perhaps are long dead . . . The
house remains to conjure up images of life
past . . . and to remind us whose life is so
present . . . that our present . . . will one day
also become the past.

The shattered glass . . . and weather-worn
wood . . . symbolized the transitoriness of life
. . . The very endurance of that old house . . .
seems to emphasize how quickly human lives
change.

Its quiet presence . . . stirs unsettling questions about how we live our present lives . . .
"What am I really living for?" . . . "What is
really important in my present life?" . . . or as
Jesus put it . . . "What profit does a man show
. . . who gains the whole world . . . and
destroys himself in the process? . . . What can
a man offer . . . in exchange for his life?"
(Mark 8:36-37).

Caring

A chill, brisk afternoon . . . in an almost empty picnic grounds . . . a woman huddles two small children close to her . . . under her protective arms . . . warming them? . . . reconciling them after a fight? . . . or just loving them?

The scene suggests Jesus' sad words to Jerusalem . . . and to all who fail in faith . . . "How often have I yearned . . . to gather your children . . . as a mother bird gathers her young under her wings . . . but you refused me" (Matthew 23:37).

Jesus' image echoes that of the Psalmist . . . who describes true faith in a caring God . . .

"You who dwell in the shelter of the Most High . . . who abide in the shadow of the Almighty . . . Say to the Lord . . . 'My refuge and my fortress . . . my God, in whom I trust' . . . With his pinions he will cover you . . . and under his wings you shall take refuge" (Psalm 91:1-4).

The Psalmist wonders aloud . . . at God's intimate care . . . and at people's total trust in so loving a God . . . "How precious is your kindness, O God! . . . The children of men take refuge in the shadow of your wings" (Psalm 36:7).

Perhaps we might pray . . . "Show your wondrous kindness, O God . . . hide me in the shadow of your wings" (Psalm 17:8).

Brothers and Sisters

Protestors march through the streets of Washington . . . Their banner proclaims their cause . . . FIGHT FOR JOBS! . . . LUCHEMOS POR TRABAJOS! . . . and their sense of solidarity . . . BROTHERS & SISTERS . . . HERMANOS Y HERMANAS.

The fact that men and women feel forced to march . . . in protest against unemployment . . . against unfair hiring practices . . . suggests the depths of suffering experienced by millions of jobless persons . . . in our cities and towns . . . on our reservations . . . and on our farms.

Their need . . . calls out for our response . . . In the fight for justice . . . we are all "Brothers & Sisters" . . . "Hermanos y Hermanas" . . . As Saint Paul teaches . . . when one member of the body suffers . . . the whole body hurts . . . and therefore he sums up the law of Jesus . . . as responding to each other's needs . . . "bearing one another's burdens" (Gal 6:2).

Jesus' call to justice and love . . . can be heard in the streets . . . and in unemployment lines . . . as well as in church . . . It can be read on protest banners . . . and anguished faces . . . as well as in the Bible . . . His command reaches us through human need and suffering . . . as well as through the Ten Commandments.

He calls us not only to pray for those in need . . . but to feel with them . . . to walk with them . . . to work with them . . . each in our own way . . . according to our abilities and opportunities . . . He calls us to love justice . . . to fight for justice . . . to recognize that we are in fact . . . BROTHERS AND SISTERS . . . HERMANOS Y HERMANAS.

others & Sisters
Hermanos y He
FIGHT
for
JOBS!
TRA
PROGRESSIVE

Peace?

People smile at each other . . . reach out their hands . . . and wish one another peace . . . Christ's peace.

All but Harry . . . Arms folded . . . jaw set . . . eyes staring straight ahead . . . he stands stoically silent and unsmiling . . . a cold symbol of closedness . . . in a setting of warm openness.

Sharing Christ's peace, to be sure . . . is not just a matter of a superficial greeting . . . or a token handshake . . . Harry may feel it is all phoney . . . He may be conservative or liberal . . . sincerely convinced or just plain stubborn . . . but his appearance becomes a chilling symbol . . . of a closed mind and heart . . . the very opposite of the openness . . . that allows for peace . . . a gift of the Holy Spirit.

The Spirit of Jesus . . . is a Spirit of peace . . . a Spirit of flexibility and adaptation . . . of strength clothed with gentleness . . . His presence bridges differences . . . blends opposites . . . melts rigidity.

The Holy Spirit brings the peace of Christ . . . to those whose hearts are open . . . whose minds are questioning . . . whose mouths can soften into a smile . . . and whose hands can reach out . . . even to those with whom one differs.

A Father's Care

A small child . . . and her father . . . out for a stroll . . . on a bright Sunday afternoon.

She seems so small . . . so unsteady on her feet . . . as if she were still learning to walk . . . Beside her and above her the father seems so large . . . so secure and agile on his feet.

Yet his eyes are constantly on her . . . his hand ready to reach out if she stumbles . . . His whole body appears poised to help . . . physically revealing his inner care and attentiveness.

The two . . . child and father . . . provide an attractive image of ourselves and God . . . our Father . . . We are in many ways fragile and insecure . . . as we boldly step out into life's unknown challenges . . . In comparison God is mighty . . . powerful beyond imagining . . . creating and sustaining the vast expanses of the universe.

Yet we believe . . . that like a father . . . His strength is at the service of His love . . . The Bible uses poetry to describe God's fatherly care . . . saying that his eyes are ever on us . . . his arm is stretched out to guide and protect us . . . his presence and his voice assuring us . . . "Fear not . . . I will be with you" (Exodus 3:12).

Locked In

Two locks . . . on a metal shield . . . covering a shop window . . . on a city street.

Locks . . . instruments of security . . . indicators of risk . . . signs of fear . . . in a world of real and imagined threats . . . against one's property . . . one's person . . . one's loved ones.

Locks . . . symbols, too . . . of spiritual closedness . . . of selfishness . . . that locks one inside oneself . . . sealed off from God . . . insensitive to others' feelings . . . irresponsive to others' needs . . . self-contained . . . self-satisfied . . . seemingly secure . . . locked inside.

To break such locks . . . of mind and spirit . . . Jesus comes to us . . . in life's joys and sorrows . . . in friends and foes . . . in the poor and hungry . . . saying . . .

"Here I stand . . . knocking at the door . . . If anyone hears me calling . . . and opens the door . . . I will enter his house . . . and have supper with him . . . and he with me" (Revelation 3:20).

Taking Aim

A young man ... muscles bulging ... draws his bow taut ... and takes careful aim ... at a distant target ...

He is a model of concentration ... of harmony between body and spirit ... Every muscle ... every nerve ... is mobilized ... to send that arrow straight to the target's center ...

His singlemindedness ... mobilizes the full potential ... of his mind and body ... The goal ... the target ... draws his whole being ... in a concentrated, tensely peaceful movement.

The young archer ... fully centered on his target ... recalls Jesus' challenge ... "remember, where your treasure is ... there your heart is also" (Matthew 6:21) ... Your target ... your treasure ... draws your heart ... mobilizes your potential for good ... or for evil.

The archer's goal is clear ... Is mine? ... Is yours? ... What is my target? ... What are you aiming at in life? ... Where is your treasure?

Jesus asks each of us over and over ... what he asked his very first followers ... "What are you looking for?" (John 1:38).

Christic is the Answer

Two black-robed nuns . . . approach a rally of youthful Jesus people . . . whose truck proclaims in paint . . . the message that gives meaning . . . to the nun's traditional way of religious life . . . and to the Jesus youths' new lifestyle . . . CHRIST IS THE ANSWER.

Two dramatically different ways . . . of responding to Jesus . . . One rooted in centuries of Church tradition . . . the other abandoning institutional ways and traditions . . . to go directly to personal experience and the Bible.

Yet nuns in black . . . and Jesus people in T-shirts and cotton dresses . . . agree on what is ultimately more important than either lifestyle . . . namely, that Christ is the answer . . .

Some scoff at the "good sisters" as irrelevant . . . while others laugh at "Jesus freaks" as irreverent . . . but the message of both has a gnawing urgency . . . CHRIST IS THE ANSWER.

The answer to what? . . . To life's deepest mysteries and questions . . . like the mystery of suffering and death . . . or the question of life's ultimate meaning . . . or the mystery of evil in the human heart . . . or questions like . . . What is love? . . . What is freedom? . . . What is peace? . . . Christ is the answer . . . to those mysteries of life . . . and those unsettling questions . . . that cannot be fully answered . . . by science . . . or philosophy . . . or money . . . or pleasure . . . or power.

Perhaps Christ is the answer . . . only for those who love life enough . . . to wonder at its mysteries . . . and probe its deeper questions . . . Some nuns are like that . . . So are some Jesus people . . . Am I? . . . Are you?

Affection

A man . . . and a woman . . . husband and wife . . . sharing an intimate moment together . . . clearly enjoying each other's presence.

An image of intimate affection . . . that reflects the happy experience of men and women . . . who share a similar relationship . . . that pulls at the hearts of others . . . who yearn to be loved by one special other . . . that surfaces the pain of many . . . whose affective bond with another has disintegrated.

A man . . . and a woman . . . united in love . . . an image, too . . . of God . . . and us, his People . . . united in a mysterious bond of affection . . . we have come to call "grace."

The Bible uses the language of love . . . romance . . . intimacy . . . to describe our grace-bond with God:

"With age-old love I have loved you" . . . our God assures us through the prophet Jeremiah (31:3).

Our response . . . secure in His faithful affection . . . is voiced by the bride in the Song of Songs . . . "My lover belongs to me . . . and I to him" (2:16; 6:3; 7:11).

Fragments

A broken shell . . . lies among unnumbered millions of shells . . . on the ocean sand . . . Once a whole, beautiful shell . . . now it is but pieces . . . fragments, broken and scattered.

A symbol of our lives.

In today's constantly changing, complex, complicated world . . . we so often feel the pain of being fragmented . . . torn . . . our lives full of cracks and pieces . . . that somehow don't hold together.

The deep yearning of our lives is for whole-ness . . . a sense of being at one . . . of having it all together.

Not unlike the blind and lame of the Gospels . . . we feel an inner cry well up in our brokenness . . . "Lord, make me whole . . . Somehow glue me back together!"

Jesus often responded . . . with a gentle touch . . . and a healing word . . . "Be whole again!"

We believe he is with us still . . . giving us his spirit . . . A Holy Spirit of wholeness and healing . . . a unifying, centering Spirit . . . to make us whole . . . at peace . . . at one.

"Lord . . . help me put the pieces of my life together . . . Help me become whole."

New Beginnings

An infant . . . lies contented on a desk . . . secure in the affectionate gaze of a loved one . . . seemingly full of vitality . . . her arms open as if to embrace the world.

A baby . . . symbol of beginnings . . . of new life . . . of renewed hope and expectation . . . For her everything is new . . . most anything seems possible . . . Her unforseeable potential waits to be actualized . . . The whole world lies open before her.

An infant is an invitation . . . to each of us . . . whatever our age . . . to allow the child yet within us . . . to grow . . . Each baby beckons us . . . to open ourselves to life . . . to begin anew . . . to try again . . . Every child challenges us . . . to uncover the unfulfilled potential . . . that lies hidden within us . . . to look at the future as full of promise . . . for growth . . . as we enter into it . . . under the loving gaze . . . of a gracious God.

A baby . . . symbolizes new opportunities . . . filled with unexpected grace . . . May we be open to them . . . like a child . . . with faith and trust.

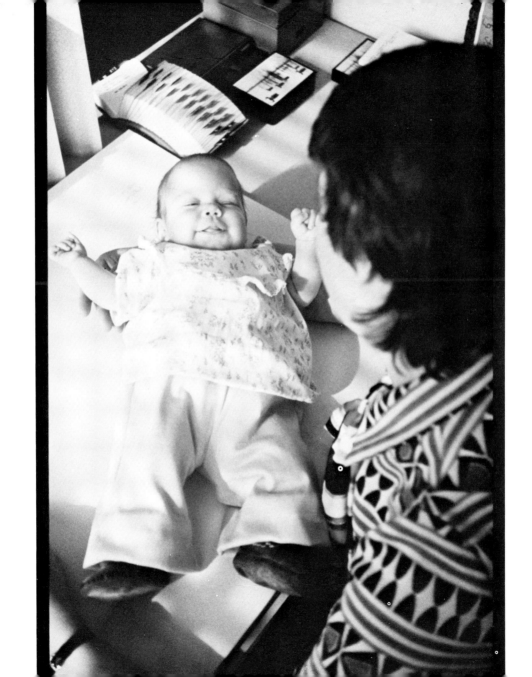

Tearing Down

Urban renewers . . . tear down a building . . . crashing into walls that once provided shelter . . . into rooms that experienced unseen acts . . . of tenderness and harshness . . . caring and disregard . . . celebration and desecration . . . life and death.

Workers paid to destroy . . . to demolish . . . what once was a sanctuary of community . . . and nurturer of creativity . . . in order to make way for new buildings . . . more hospitable to people . . . more stimulating of creativity . . . With their steel instruments of destruction . . . they tear down . . . to build up.

The dust rising from the rubbled walls . . . chokes one with sadness . . . for something has died . . . but the cleared space . . . expands one's heart . . . to sense possibilities for new life . . . latent in the scarred space.

Tearing down . . . is part of every upbuilding . . . in renewing cities . . . and people . . . Dying contains seeds of new life . . . which blossoms only through death.

As God sent His prophet Jeremiah . . . so he sends each of us . . . into our own hearts . . . and into our world . . .

"to root up and to tear down,
to destroy and demolish,
to build and to plant"

(Jeremiah 1:10).

Pieta

A son's death . . . A mother's grief. He lies limp . . . emptied of life . . . executed as a criminal . . . on a cross . . . outside the city . . . his left hand cramped around a nail's raw wound.

She kneels in grief . . . hurting . . . helpless . . . her arms stretched out . . . in anguish . . . in acceptance . . . her face pained . . . but peaceful.

Her mind asks . . . like millions of mothers . . . before and since . . . "Why?" . . . "Why my son?"

No reasoned answer comes . . . Death's mystery escapes the limits of the human mind . . . Only the heart can enter death's darkness . . . and there find light . . . life . . .

Only the heart of one . . . like Mary . . . who knows the living God . . . as a gracious God . . . whose life-giving love . . . creates new life . . . out of death's tears.

Her heart . . . full of trust . . . responds now . . . as once she prayed in a happier hour . . .

"I am the servant of the Lord . . . " (Luke 1:38)

Listening

A boy . . . and a man . . . deep in conversation . . . It is not important if the man is the boy's father, or brother, coach, teacher, or friend . . . What is important is their absorption in their conversation.

The boy seems at ease . . . talking . . . He looks happy . . . The man listens . . . somewhat serious . . . but relaxed . . . There is a feeling of mutual trust . . . a sense of peaceful understanding . . . a respectful sharing.

It's not often one sees someone genuinely listening to another . . . Even rarer is the sight of an adult really listening to a child . . . taking a child seriously . . . as having something to say.

When is the last time you felt someone listened to you? . . . really listened?

Listening to another says . . . "You're important to me" . . . "You have something worth saying" . . . "You're worth my time and attention" . . . "You're O.K."

True listening frees one to be oneself . . . to reveal one's weaker self . . . to want to become one's better self . . . Hardly anything is more healing . . . more creative . . . more loving.

The boy is lucky . . . to have found someone who really listens . . . No wonder he talks happily . . . at peace.

Freedom's Price

An old graveyard . . . from Revolutionary War days . . . gravestones cracked and crumbling after 200 years . . . quiet monuments to felled freedom fighters.

The flag . . . hanging listlessly in the breezeless afternoon . . . celebrates the freedom . . . for which these men died . . . and their families suffered.

We gaze at their graves . . . free men and women . . . free because they counted dying in freedom . . . worth more than living under oppression.

Was it worth their lives? . . . Is our freedom that valuable?

The sight of their graves . . . the memory of their values and deeds . . . stirs feelings of admiration . . . and thanks . . . and surfaces challenging questions . . . about freedom's worth . . . and freedom's price.

What does it mean to us to be free? . . . How do we measure the value of freedom? . . . Do we do as much to keep it . . . as they did to win it for us? . . . What are we willing to do . . . to guarantee every American a full share in those freedoms . . . the worth of which these stones silently suggest?

Meditation

Three teenagers . . . sit peacefully on the living room floor . . . together yet each alone . . . deep in meditation.

Meditation . . . an ancient art . . . rediscovered by the young . . . a Catholic tradition . . . common to all great faiths . . . a searching, centering experience . . . shared by all seekers of peace and meaning . . . whether believers or not.

To meditate is . . . to stop flitting across the surface of life . . . to take time to gaze into one's heart . . . and to search the depths of things . . . to still the turmoil . . . and order the clutter . . . that fence us off . . . from ultimate reality.

To meditate is . . . to open one's mind and heart . . . to the unsuspected depths of daily life . . . to free one's inner eye . . . to see life's inner meaning . . . to empty oneself . . . so as to be filled with God's gifts . . . of Light . . . and Life . . . and Love.

"Pause a while," . . . invites the Lord . . . "and know that I am God" (Psalm 46:10).

Reaching

A man . . . reaching up . . . straining for what is beyond his grasp . . . stretching for something more . . . something higher . . . greater.

This famous statue in downtown Cleveland . . . symbolizes the yearning . . . of the human heart . . . ever to excel . . . to find its fulfillment . . . outside the confines . . . of what can be grasped . . . held . . . manipulated.

Something in the human heart . . . yearns for the infinite . . . for something . . . Someone . . . greater than itself . . . greater even than its dreams.

One's reach . . . needs ever to extend beyond one's grasp . . . not for more acquisitions . . . pleasure . . . power . . . but for greater growth . . . greater openness . . . lest one become self-satisfied . . . sated . . . dulled to life's mystery.

"Seek" . . . says the Lord . . . "and you shall find . . . for everyone who seeks . . . finds" (Matthew 7:8).

Like Children

Two young friends . . . huddled close . . . full of eagerness and anticipation . . . are an attractive image of the youthful openness and togetherness . . . Jesus called "poverty of spirit."

Jesus praised as "happy" . . . those spiritually poor . . . that is . . . those with the hearts of youngsters . . . open to the riches of life . . . and life's surprises . . . aware of their need for others . . . expectant of meeting their God . . . in the most usual happenings.

Poverty of spirit is a youthful spirit . . . still able to wonder . . . at the extraordinary in the ordinary . . . as mystery breaks through monotony . . . as old answers spark deeper questions . . . as life wins out over death . . . It is a warm spirit . . . creative of closeness . . . bonding with others in affection and concern.

Only such people . . . says Jesus . . . those like children . . . are at home in his Father's house (Matthew 5:3; 19:13).

Freedom

A young black man stands reverently . . . at the grave of Martin Luther King, Jr. . . . in Atlanta, Georgia . . . A gentle flame burns continually . . . recalling the undying spirit of a man . . . whose love of freedom . . . led to a tragic, violent, early death.

His tombstone proclaims his final possession . . . of the full freedom that eluded him . . . and all of us . . . during life . . . "Free at last . . . Thank God Almighty, I'm free at last."

The epitaph suggests a challenging reality . . . that death is always the price of freedom . . . Only in dying can we find real freedom.

We are all slaves . . . held by chains that bind our minds and spirits . . . chains of selfishness and fear . . . chains that bind us to pettiness . . . jealousy . . . injustice . . . even hate . . . chains that St. Paul calls "Sin."

From these chains there is no freedom . . . except in dying . . . dying to the selfishness that keeps us from caring about others . . . dying to the fear that drains us of courage . . . dying to the blindness that dims our vision of other's needs.

Such daily dying . . . frees one to care . . . to reach out with compassion . . . to listen with sensitivity . . . to stand up and fight for justice . . . to face physical death with confident hope . . . of fuller life and freedom . . . "Unless the seed die" . . . Jesus said . . . "it remains barren . . . but if it dies . . . it bears rich fruit" (John 12:24).

Confrontation

A confrontation on a city street . . . between police . . . and young Jewish demonstrators . . . protesting Russian emigration policies . . . The youths sit in a normally busy downtown intersection . . . halting traffic . . . The police move in . . . to move the demonstrators out . . . It is all peaceful . . . but serious . . . It is a question of freedom.

"Let my people go," echoes Moses' challenge to Egypt's Pharaoh . . . 32 centuries ago . . . Like Pharaoh the police stand firm . . . their steel truck symbolizing strength . . . David's star calls to mind over 3,000 years of tradition . . . among a people born in a march toward freedom . . . under the guidance of a God . . . who loves freedom.

The police, too, stand for freedom . . . for people's rights to use city streets . . . to move about where they wish . . . The police badges symbolize a government . . . born in a revolutionary battle for freedom . . . a nation proud of 200 years of freedom under law . . . the "land of the free."

The confrontation suggests very real questions . . . Who is really free? . . . What is true freedom? . . . How do people become free? . . . What is the legitimate use of force in seeking freedom? . . . How preserve freedom? . . . Questions worth pondering . . . in the light of our centuries old Judaeo-Christian tradition . . . and our more recent 200 years experience as a nation . . . in the light of Jesus Christ . . . who came to set us all free.

Jesus is Lord

A busy street . . . a downtown university campus . . . people on their way to class or work.

Above them is posted . . . on two huge signs . . . someone's profession of faith . . . "Lord" . . . "Jesus."

This most ancient profession of faith in Jesus Christ . . . "Jesus is Lord!" (Romans 11:9; I Corinthians 12:3) . . . dominates this contemporary urban scene . . . The very ordinariness of the situation . . . suggests the real meaning . . . of so extraordinary a belief.

For to confess Jesus as Lord . . . is to believe He is present . . . with gentle power . . . with saving strength . . . in people's hearts as they live their daily lives . . . on city streets . . . on campuses and in offices . . . in factories and on farms . . . everywhere . . . always.

To proclaim Jesus as Lord . . . affirms that His presence . . . makes a decisive difference . . . in all of life . . . that His influence gives meaning and direction to everyday living . . . that He is the key that unlocks life's mystery.

"Lord" . . . "Jesus" . . . Bold signs . . . calling us to follow St. Paul's urging . . . "Continue to live in Christ Jesus the Lord . . . Be rooted in Him . . . and built up in Him . . . growing ever stronger in faith . . . as you were taught . . . and overflowing with gratitude" (Colossians 2:6-7).

Broken

A broken window . . . with fragments of shattered glass . . . held to its weather-worn frame by dried, cracked putty . . . It stands out starkly . . . with its whites and grays . . . against a solid black emptiness.

It looks like a cross . . . It jars us to look again at Christ's cross . . . and our own lives.

So much of life seems broken . . . People speak of human existence as somehow fractured . . . We all feel the cuts . . . of life's sharp, brittle edges.

Christians have long pondered the brokenness of life . . . They call it "original sin" . . . or "sinfulness" . . . or simply "Sin" . . . Whatever the theological term . . . we ex-perience the shattered . . . and the shriveled . . . inside ourselves . . . and all around us.

Surprisingly . . . Christians have just as long believed . . . that their Father, God . . . lovingly sent his only Son . . . to enter fully into our broken world . . . to be broken Himself . . . to be cut on life's sharp edges . . . to share fully our hurt . . . That's the cross . . . crucifixion!

But why? . . . To show us that the deepest of all cuts . . . can be healed . . . that the most brittle can again become supple . . . that cracks can bond into new unity . . . that the broken can be made whole.

The cross of Jesus keeps telling us . . . through all its painful realism . . . that the very brokenness of life . . . contains the seeds of wholeness . . . and renewed life . . . life's light . . . visible in the cross.

Mother and Child

A mother . . . and her child . . . together in a quiet moment . . . smiling . . . enjoying being together . . . taken up with each other . . . united in affection and trust.

A beautiful sight . . . a warm human experience . . . close to the heart of what life is all about . . . but a profound symbol as well . . . of an even deeper relationship . . . that between God and each of us.

The Bible speaks of God as a mother . . . as well as a father . . . The prophet Hosea has God say affectionately of us, his people . . . "It was I who took them in my arms . . . I drew them with human cords . . . with bonds of love . . . I cared for them like one who raises an infant to his cheeks" (Hosea 11:3-5).

God loves us as this mother loves her son . . . actually even more than any mother . . . The prophet Isaiah portrays God saying . . .

"Can a mother forget her infant, be without tenderness for the child of her womb? . . . Even if she forgets, I will never forget you" (Isaiah 49:15).

One has to be like a child really to believe that . . . Maybe that is why Jesus once took a child . . . placed him before his followers . . . and told them that unless they became like that little child . . . they could not enter God's kingdom . . . nor even begin to wonder at the profound reality . . . that so great a God . . . loved them with a mother's tenderness . . . and fidelity.

For Jesus . . . and the prophets before him . . . the symbol of the true believer . . . is a little child . . . like this small boy . . . smiling confidently at his mother . . . knowing that she loves him . . . trusting that she cares . . . at peace in her presence.

It may seem a paradox . . . It is certainly a mystery . . . God, the all powerful, loves like a mother . . . A mature believer . . . trusts like a child.

Grace and Faith

An Oriental child—a Western mother . . . two cultures bridged in a gesture of love . . . The little girl seems apprehensive . . . shy . . . uncomfortable . . . half-trusting . . . half wondering what will happen next . . . looking aside . . . her big eyes questioning . . . in spite of the mother's love.

God's love or grace . . . and human faith . . . are like that . . . full of wonder . . . of mystery . . . The prophet Hosea tells us about God's grace . . . He has God saying . . . "I drew them with human cords . . . with bands of love . . . I fostered them like one who raises an infant to His cheeks" (Hosea 11:4) . . .

God's love or grace . . . reaches out to us . . . bridging the vast chasm between Himself and us . . . lifting us in an embrace of love . . . like a mother or father . . . holding a loved child.

God's gracious generosity invites our trust . . . or faith . . . which the Bible likens to that of a child . . . in its mother's arms . . . Aware of its need . . . a child trusts in the love and strength of someone greater . . . But like many children . . . we seem always to wonder . . . to question . . . to doubt . . . "Can it be true? . . . Why should God care about me?"

Jesus' message to us repeats over and over . . . "Yes, it is true! . . . Why are you afraid? . . . Why do you doubt? . . . You of little faith!" . . . Jesus assures us . . . that in spite of the gulf between the all-holy God . . . who is our Father . . . or Mother . . . amazing as it seems . . . we are God's children . . . freely adopted . . . held close by bonds of unchanging love.

Like the man in the Gospel . . . astonished at the marvel of God's love . . . and aware of his weak faith . . . we can pray . . . "Lord, I do believe . . . Help my unbelief!" (Mark 9:24).

Lovers

Two young lovers . . . walk along together . . . absorbed in one another . . . as they round a bend . . . and walk into a woods.

Where does their path lead? . . . What lies around the bend of life's winding path? . . . What does their future hold?

What lies ahead . . . remains hidden from them . . . What is to come . . . is veiled with uncertainty . . . What awaits them in life's shadowed woods . . . cannot be guessed.

But they walk into the unknown . . . together . . . trusting in their mutual love . . . as source of strength . . . as unfailing guide . . . as grounds for hope.

Love is all that . . . Love is stronger than life's fiercest obstacles . . . surer guide than reason . . . a firmer ground of hope than power . . . or riches.

For love . . . partakes of God . . . who is life's surest ground . . . and unfailing light.

"Love bears all . . . believes all . . . hopes for everything . . . endures all things . . . Love never fails" (I Corinthians 13:7).